DR. DENNY BATES

My Spiritual Life Plan:

Creating An Effective Spiritual Life Plan
For The Quality Disciple

An Assessment And Implementation Of Eight Core Essentials

For Disciples Of Jesus

A Quality Disciple Resource

A Quality Disciple . . . A Quality Life

QUALITY
LEADERSHIP CONSULTANTS

My Spiritual Life Plan:

Creating An Effective Spiritual Life Plan
For The Quality Disciple

An Assessment Of Eight Core Essentials Of A Disciple Of Jesus

A Quality Disciple . . . A Quality Life

Dr. Denny Bates

Dr. Denny Bates & Something New Christian Publishers © 2013
www.dennybates.com

QUALITY
LEADERSHIP CONSULTANTS

My Spiritual Life Plan:

Creating An Effective Spiritual Life Plan
For The Quality Disciple

Something New Christian Publishers

E-Mail dennybates@gmail.com

On the Web: www.dennybates.com

or visit my teaching blog at

http://thequalitydisciple.blogspot.com

or you can "friend" me on Facebook at www.facebook.com/denny.bates

or follow me on Twitter @dennybates

QUALITY
LEADERSHIP CONSULTANTS

Table of Contents

Dr. Denny Bates & Something New Christian Publishers © 2013
www.dennybates.com

Spiritual Growth Practices Assessment
"What I Do: What I Believe & Why I Believe"

"For Ezra had set his heart to study the Law of the Lord, and to do it and to teach His statutes and rules in Israel." Ezra 7:10

On the following pages are selected biblical facts about the core values of **Grace, Worship, Bible Study, Prayer, Community, Service** and **Evangelism**. This assessment is divided into two sections: An overview of what you believe and a Biblical inquiry for why you believe. An assessment on **Discipleship** is also included. Please give your honest assessment for each statement. Use the scale of "I strongly disagree" to "I strongly agree." Select the best answer for each statement. Remember: do not give what you feel is the "right" answer. What is typical of your experience? Give the answer that is true about you today. When you have completed this exercise, consider sharing your results with another believer and/or with your small group. I've suggested many follow up questions for each one of these core values that are great prompters for an even deeper learning experience.

Everyone needs a system, a plan to learn from the past in order to set achievable goals in the future. You are invited to assess where you have been, where you are and where you wish to go.

Ready to begin? Take some time to pray and invite the Lord to speak to you throughout this exercise. In your hands is not only an assessment tool, but also a unique kind of spiritual exercise. You will soon discover that this will be a meaningful, spiritual experience, and the Lord willing, a chance for spiritual growth to occur—even as you take this assessment.

Are you ready? Are you set? Let's GROW!

[11] Dear brothers and sisters, I close my letter with these last words: Be joyful. Grow to maturity. Encourage each other. Live in harmony and peace. Then the God of love and peace will be with you. **2 Corinthians 13:11 (NLT)**

[15] Rather, let our lives lovingly express truth [in all things, speaking truly, dealing truly, living truly]. Enfolded in love, let us grow up in every way *and* in all things into Him Who is the Head, [even] Christ (the Messiah, the Anointed One). **Ephesians 4:15 (AMP)**

[15] God wants us to grow up, to know the whole truth and tell it in love—like Christ in everything. We take our lead from Christ, who is the source of everything we do. **Ephesians 4:15 (MSG)**

[18] But grow in grace (undeserved favor, spiritual strength) and recognition *and* knowledge *and* understanding of our Lord and Savior Jesus Christ (the Messiah). To Him [be] glory (honor, majesty, and splendor) both now and to the day of eternity. Amen (so be it)! **2 Peter 3:18 (AMP)**

GRACE: (An Overview of What I Believe)

"The law detects, grace alone conquers sin." ~ Saint Augustine of Hippo (354-430)

"A man can no more take in a supply of grace for the future than he can eat enough today to last him for the next 6 months, nor can he inhale sufficient air into his lungs with one breath to sustain life for a week to come. We are permitted to draw upon God's store of grace from day to day as we need it." ~ D. L. Moody

"God, give us grace to accept with serenity the things that cannot be changed, courage to change the things that can be changed, and the wisdom to distinguish one from the other" ~ Reinhold Niebuhr (American theologian)

I put more trust in God than I do in myself

1	2	3	4	5
Strongly Disagree	Disagree	Somewhat Agree	Agree	Strongly Agree

I believe that I am saved by grace, and by grace alone

1	2	3	4	5
Strongly Disagree	Disagree	Somewhat Agree	Agree	Strongly Agree

It is my habit to give away grace to those who do not deserve it

1	2	3	4	5
Strongly Disagree	Disagree	Somewhat Agree	Agree	Strongly Agree

I walk in forgiveness of my sins, not in crushing guilt and self-condemnation

1	2	3	4	5
Strongly Disagree	Disagree	Somewhat Agree	Agree	Strongly Agree

I am growing in the grace and knowledge of Jesus Christ

1	2	3	4	5
Strongly Disagree	Disagree	Somewhat Agree	Agree	Strongly Agree

GRACE: (A Biblical Inquiry For Why I Believe)

1.   I am Saved by Grace

[8] For it is by grace you have been saved, through faith--and this not from yourselves, it is the gift of God--[9] not by works, so that no one can boast. **Ephesians 2:8-9**

1	2	3	4	5
I strongly disagree	I somewhat disagree	I somewhat agree	I agree	I strongly agree

How has the grace of God transformed your life?

When is it the most challenging for you to live in grace?

What kind of advice would you give the person who has great difficulty in escaping the snares of legalism and the law?

2.   It has been my experience to receive one blessing after another

From the fullness of his grace we have all received one blessing after another. **John 1:16**

1	2	3	4	5
I strongly disagree	I somewhat disagree	I somewhat agree	I agree	I strongly agree

What has been your experience when you talk about God's blessings in your life?

Has there ever been a hindrance that prevented you from walking in the fullness of God's grace?

What kind of advice would you give the person who desires abundant blessings from the Lord?

3.   **It has been my experience to be driven by love, not performance**

For sin shall not be your master, because you are not under law, but under grace.
Romans 6:14

1	2	3	4	5
I strongly disagree	I somewhat disagree	I somewhat agree	I agree	I strongly agree

How does God's grace impact on the way you feel about yourself?

Is there anything in your life that hinders you from being free from habitual sin?

How does the grace of God, in your life, keep you from falling into the performance trap?

What kind of advice would you give the person who is trapped in a life of habitual sin and cannot break free?

4.   It has been my experience to have help in my time of need

Let us then approach the throne of grace with confidence, so that we may receive mercy and find grace to help us in our time of need. **Hebrews 4:16**

1	2	3	4	5
I strongly disagree	I somewhat disagree	I somewhat agree	I agree	I strongly agree

What is your attitude concerning how free you are in approaching God's throne with your needs?

How does having the opportunity to approach this Throne of Grace impact you on a daily basis?

What kind of advice would you give the person who is desperate and in great need?

5. **It has been my experience to have my faith and love magnified**

[14] The grace of our Lord was poured out on me abundantly, along with the faith and love that are in Christ Jesus. **1 Timothy 1:14**

1	2	3	4	5
I strongly disagree	I somewhat disagree	I somewhat agree	I agree	I strongly agree

How do you position yourself in order to experience grace being poured out on you abundantly?

How does the connection of grace in your life magnify your faith and love?

What kind of advice would you give the person who seemed to be missing out on an abundance of grace and faith and love?

More Thoughts And Action Steps On Grace:

1. Write a clear and precise description of what it will mean for you to grow in grace this year.

2. Then, make a list of the specific goals you need to experience for growth in grace (You are now going from "what it means for you" to "what will make it possible" for you to achieve success)

3. With each specific goal you list above, list the steps you will need to achieve in order to reach your goal.

4. Then, list the tasks that will be required to take each step.

5. Then, set a schedule of beginning and completion dates for each task and step

6. Finally, who will hold you accountable to reach your spiritual goals?

WORSHIP: (An Overview of What I Believe)

"The most eloquent prayer is the prayer through hands that heal and bless. The highest form of worship is the worship of unselfish Christian service. The greatest form of praise is the sound of consecrated feet seeking out the lost and helpless." ~ Billy Graham

God is most glorified in us, when we are most satisfied in Him. ~ John Piper

The most valuable thing the Pslams do for me is to express that same delight in God which made David dance. ~ C.S. Lewis

My worship of God is not based upon how I "feel" but by faith

1	2	3	4	5
Strongly Disagree	Disagree	Somewhat Agree	Agree	Strongly Agree

I have no idols in my life that compromise my worship of God and God alone

1	2	3	4	5
Strongly Disagree	Disagree	Somewhat Agree	Agree	Strongly Agree

I know how to please God with my worship of Him

1	2	3	4	5
Strongly Disagree	Disagree	Somewhat Agree	Agree	Strongly Agree

I am in awe of God when I worship Him

1	2	3	4	5
Strongly Disagree	Disagree	Somewhat Agree	Agree	Strongly Agree

I am giving my life away for the Lord as I offer my body as a living sacrifice to God

1	2	3	4	5
Strongly Disagree	Disagree	Somewhat Agree	Agree	Strongly Agree

WORSHIP: (A Biblical Inquiry For Why I Believe)

1.   **My worship of God is an act of faith**

He said to his servants, "Stay here with the donkey while I and the boy go over there. We will worship and then we will come back to you." **Genesis 22:5**

1	2	3	4	5
I strongly disagree	I somewhat disagree	I somewhat agree	I agree	I strongly agree

Can you recall an example of when you had to worship God by faith?

What kind of advice would you give the person who has a hard time worshiping a God he or she cannot see (and sometimes, even "feel")?

2.   It has been my experience to give my worship exclusively to God and to God alone

Do not worship any other god, for the LORD, whose name is Jealous, is a jealous God. **Exodus 34:14**

1	2	3	4	5
I strongly disagree	I somewhat disagree	I somewhat agree	I agree	I strongly agree

What has been the catalyst to you from having fidelity in your worship?

What has been the hindrance that keeps you from giving God all of your worship?

What kind of advice would you give the person who does not give God all of his or her worship?

3.   **It has been my experience to worship God in a way that pleases Him**

ascribe to the LORD the glory due his name. Bring an offering and come before him; worship the LORD in the splendor of his holiness. **1 Chronicles 16:29**

1	2	3	4	5
I strongly disagree	I somewhat disagree	I somewhat agree	I agree	I strongly agree

How do you know when you are pleasing God with your worship?

What kind of advice would you give the person who sincerely wanted to know what kind of worship pleases the Lord?

4.   My worship of God brings to me an incredible sense of humility

[6] Come, let us bow down in worship, let us kneel before the LORD our Maker; [7] for he is our God and we are the people of his pasture, the flock under his care. Today, if you hear his voice, **Psalms 95:6-7**

1	2	3	4	5
I strongly disagree	I somewhat disagree	I somewhat agree	I agree	I strongly agree

How does your worship of God give you perspective of how you approach and relate to Him?

What has been your greatest challenge when it comes to approaching God in worship?

What kind of advice would you give to the person who wanted to know how God wants to be approached?

5. **When I worship God I often want to experience God in an awesome way**

Worship the LORD in the splendor of his holiness; tremble before him, all the earth.
Psalms 96:9

1	2	3	4	5
I strongly disagree	I somewhat disagree	I somewhat agree	I agree	I strongly agree

How much passion do you bring in your worship of God?

After you worship God how does it make you feel when you are done?

What kind of advice would you give to the person who wanted not to only *know* that God exists, but wants to *experience* Him as well?

More Thoughts And Action Steps On Worship:

1. Write a clear and precise description of what it will mean for you to grow in worship this year.

2. Then, make a list of the specific goals you need to experience for growth in worship (You are now going from "what it means for you" to "what will make it possible" for you to achieve success)

3. With each specific goal you list above, list the steps you will need to achieve in order to reach your goal.

4. Then, list the tasks that will be required to take each step.

5. Then, set a schedule of beginning and completion dates for each task and step

6. Finally, who will hold you accountable to reach your spiritual goals?

BIBLE STUDY: (An Overview of What I Believe)

If you see a Bible that is falling apart, it probably belongs to someone who isn't! ~ Vance Havner

The Bible is like a telescope. If a man looks through his telescope, then he sees the worlds beyond; but if he looks at his telescope, then he does not see anything but that. The Bible is a thing to be looked through, to see that which is beyond; but most people only look at it; and so they see only the dead letter. ~ Phillips Brooks

We may be certain that whatever God has made prominent in his word, he intended to be conspicuous in our lives. ~ Charles Spurgeon

---

I read my Bible every day *and* take the time to reflect upon it

1	2	3	4	5
Strongly Disagree	Disagree	Somewhat Agree	Agree	Strongly Agree

I often find direction for my life when I study God's Word

1	2	3	4	5
Strongly Disagree	Disagree	Somewhat Agree	Agree	Strongly Agree

I feel confident in my ability to study God's Word correctly and get something I can use

1	2	3	4	5
Strongly Disagree	Disagree	Somewhat Agree	Agree	Strongly Agree

I seek to memorize portions of the Bible

1	2	3	4	5
Strongly Disagree	Disagree	Somewhat Agree	Agree	Strongly Agree

---

I have a good grasp of the major themes, doctrines, stories, and books of the Bible

1	2	3	4	5
Strongly Disagree	Disagree	Somewhat Agree	Agree	Strongly Agree

BIBLE STUDY: (A Biblical Inquiry For Why I Believe)

1.   **It is often my experience to soak my heart in the Scriptures**

Let the word of Christ dwell in you richly as you teach and admonish one another with all wisdom, and as you sing psalms, hymns and spiritual songs with gratitude in your hearts to God. **Col. 3:16**

1	2	3	4	5
I strongly disagree	I somewhat disagree	I somewhat agree	I agree	I strongly agree

What is your plan that allows the Scriptures to soak your heart?

How is your typical day best described after spending quality time in God's Word?

What kind of advice would you give the person who had no desire to spend time in God's Word?

2.   I look to God's Word for direction

Your word is a lamp to my feet and a light for my path. **Psalms 119:105**

1	2	3	4	5
I strongly disagree	I somewhat disagree	I somewhat agree	I agree	I strongly agree

Can you think of a recent example when you received divine guidance after spending time in God's Word?

When you approach God's Word for direction, where do you begin?

What kind of advice would you give the person who was lacking comfort and direction in life?

3.   **I often find myself being built up after studying God's Word**

"Now I commit you to God and to the word of his grace, which can build you up and give you an inheritance among all those who are sanctified. **Acts 20:32**

1	2	3	4	5
I strongly disagree	I somewhat disagree	I somewhat agree	I agree	I strongly agree

Can you think of a time when after reading and studying God's Word, you walked away encouraged?

What kinds of things are hindrances to you when you are discouraged which keep you from being encouraged?

What kind of advice would you give the person who needs to be built up and encouraged?

4.   It is often my practice to keep the Scriptures on the forefront of my mind

Do not let this Book of the Law depart from your mouth; meditate on it day and night, so that you may be careful to do everything written in it. Then you will be prosperous and successful. **Joshua 1:8**

1	2	3	4	5
I strongly disagree	I somewhat disagree	I somewhat agree	I agree	I strongly agree

What is your strategy when it comes to keeping God's Word on the forefront of your mind?

What challenges do you face when seeking to faithfully live out what you know to be the truth of God's commands?

Can you think of time where after spending quality time in God's Word it caused you to be prosperous and successful? Share an example and what you learned.

What kind of advice would you give the person who has no desire to either memorize or at the very least become intimately familiar with the Scriptures?

5. **I have great delight when I read God's Word**

But his delight is in the law of the LORD, and on his law he meditates day and night.
Psalms 1:2

1	2	3	4	5
I strongly disagree	I somewhat disagree	I somewhat agree	I agree	I strongly agree

When you meditate upon the Scriptures, what kinds of things do you think about or do?

What is your greatest challenge when it comes to filling your mind with the Word of God?

What kind of advice would you give to the person who does not how to meditate on the Word of God?

More Thoughts And Action Steps On Bible Study:

1. Write a clear and precise description of what it will mean for you to grow in Bible study this year.

2. Then, make a list of the specific goals you need to experience for growth in Bible study (You are now going from "what it means for you" to "what will make it possible" for you to achieve success)

3. With each specific goal you list above, list the steps you will need to achieve in order to reach your goal.

4. Then, list the tasks that will be required to take each step.

5. Then, set a schedule of beginning and completion dates for each task and step

6. Finally, who will hold you accountable to reach your spiritual goals?

PRAYER: (An Overview of What I Believe)

When a Christian shuns fellowship with other Christians, the devil smiles. When he stops studying the Bible, the devil laughs. When he stops praying, the devil shouts for joy. ~ Corrie ten Boom

We pray for the big things and forget to give thanks for the ordinary, small (and yet not so small) gifts. How can God entrust great things to one who will not thankfully receive from Him the little things? ~ Dietrich Bonhoeffer

A man prayed, and at first he thought that prayer was talking. But he became more quiet until in the end he realized that prayer is listening. ~ Soren Kierkegaard

---

I talk to God every day

1	2	3	4	5
Strongly Disagree	Disagree	Somewhat Agree	Agree	Strongly Agree

I listen for God's voice before I make an important decision

1	2	3	4	5
Strongly Disagree	Disagree	Somewhat Agree	Agree	Strongly Agree

I make it a point to regularly confess my sins to God

1	2	3	4	5
Strongly Disagree	Disagree	Somewhat Agree	Agree	Strongly Agree

I pray with a small group of other believers

1	2	3	4	5
Strongly Disagree	Disagree	Somewhat Agree	Agree	Strongly Agree

---

I pray for missionaries

1	2	3	4	5
Strongly Disagree	Disagree	Somewhat Agree	Agree	Strongly Agree

PRAYER: (A Biblical Inquiry For Why I Believe)

1.   My prayer life is like a love language I have for the Lord

[1] I love the LORD, for he heard my voice; he heard my cry for mercy. [2] Because he turned his ear to me, I will call on him as long as I live. **Psalms 116:1-2**

1	2	3	4	5
I strongly disagree	I somewhat disagree	I somewhat agree	I agree	I strongly agree

Would you describe my prayer life as one of intimacy or one of ritual and religious duty?

How do you know that the Lord is listening to your voice?

What kinds of coaching tips would you give the young believer who is still trying to find their "voice" in prayer?

2.   For me, prayer is a habit (a spiritual discipline) that I live out on a regular basis

[17] pray continually; **1 Thessalonians 5:17**

1	2	3	4	5
I strongly disagree	I somewhat disagree	I somewhat agree	I agree	I strongly agree

What do you think it means to "pray continually?"

What would you have to do in your personal life in order to deepen your prayer life?

What one thing would you share with a new believer who is struggling to develop a life of prayer?

3. **When I pray, I believe the Lord will answer me in a powerful way**

[15] He will call upon me, and I will answer him; I will be with him in trouble, I will deliver him and honor him. **Psalms 91:15**

1	2	3	4	5
I strongly disagree	I somewhat disagree	I somewhat agree	I agree	I strongly agree

When you pray, do you believe your problems are bigger than God or do you believe that God is bigger than your problems?

Describe a time when God did a miracle in your life as a result of your prayer to Him.

What could you say to the believer who was skeptical in the power of prayer?

4.   I do not make any major life decisions without asking the Lord for His guidance

[6] in all your ways acknowledge him, and he will make your paths straight. **Proverbs 3:6**

1	2	3	4	5
I strongly disagree	I somewhat disagree	I somewhat agree	I agree	I strongly agree

Describe the process you go through when you have to make an important decision.

When making a decision, what does it mean for you to "in all your ways acknowledge Him?"

What kind of encouragement would you give to the person who facing a fork in the road?

5. **I have discovered that my first prayer request is not always the one the Lord answers**

[8] Three times I pleaded with the Lord to take it away from me. [9] But he said to me, "My grace is sufficient for you, for my power is made perfect in weakness." Therefore I will boast all the more gladly about my weaknesses, so that Christ's power may rest on me. **2 Corinthians 12:8-9**

1	2	3	4	5
I strongly disagree	I somewhat disagree	I somewhat agree	I agree	I strongly agree

What spiritual lessons have you learned when your prayers appear to be unanswered; either / or when and how you wished?

When you are facing a crisis (physical, emotional, spiritual, etc.) how do you determine for what to pray?

What kind of counsel would you give the person who has been disappointed in God's "failure" to give them what they wanted?

More Thoughts And Action Steps On Prayer:

1. Write a clear and precise description of what it will mean for you to grow in prayer this year.

2. Then, make a list of the specific goals you need to experience for growth in prayer (You are now going from "what it means for you" to "what will make it possible" for you to achieve success)

3. With each specific goal you list above, list the steps you will need to achieve in order to reach your goal.

4. Then, list the tasks that will be required to take each step.

5. Then, set a schedule of beginning and completion dates for each task and step

6. Finally, who will hold you accountable to reach your spiritual goals?

COMMUNITY: (An Overview of What I Believe)

If a man cannot be a Christian in the place where he lives, he cannot be a Christian anywhere. ~ Henry Ward Beecher

We are long on membership but short on discipleship. We are more anxious to gather statistics than to grow saints. ~ Vance Havner

The thermometer of a church is its prayer meeting. ~ Vance Havner

This is our real "Program": faith in Christ, fellowship with Christ, faithfulness to Christ, fruitfulness for Christ. ~ Richard Baxter

---

I am an active participant in a small group

1	2	3	4	5
Strongly Disagree	Disagree	Somewhat Agree	Agree	Strongly Agree

I belong to a group where I feel safe to let them know the "real me"

1	2	3	4	5
Strongly Disagree	Disagree	Somewhat Agree	Agree	Strongly Agree

I have someone in my life that I consider to be a "mentor" to me

1	2	3	4	5
Strongly Disagree	Disagree	Somewhat Agree	Agree	Strongly Agree

I have someone in my life that I am considered to be a "mentor" to them

1	2	3	4	5
Strongly Disagree	Disagree	Somewhat Agree	Agree	Strongly Agree

---

I have a circle of friends who hold me accountable as I live out my Christian faith

1	2	3	4	5
Strongly Disagree	Disagree	Somewhat Agree	Agree	Strongly Agree

COMMUNITY: (A Biblical Inquiry For Why I Believe)

1.   Those who know me know that I have been marked by the love I have for other believers

[34] "A new command I give you: Love one another. As I have loved you, so you must love one another. [35] By this all men will know that you are my disciples, if you love one another." **John 13:34-35**

1	2	3	4	5
I strongly disagree	I somewhat disagree	I somewhat agree	I agree	I strongly agree

When you "love one another", what does that typically look like? What does love look like for those who are being loved by you?

When are you most willing to love others?

How would you model loving one another to a person who has a hard time receiving love?

2.   I am an integral part of the Body of Christ that is healthy and growing

[42] They devoted themselves to the apostles' teaching and to the fellowship, to the breaking of bread and to prayer. [43] Everyone was filled with awe, and many wonders and miraculous signs were done by the apostles. [44] All the believers were together and had everything in common. [45] Selling their possessions and goods, they gave to anyone as he had need. [46] Every day they continued to meet together in the temple courts. They broke bread in their homes and ate together with glad and sincere hearts, [47] praising God and enjoying the favor of all the people. And the Lord added to their number daily those who were being saved. **Acts 2:42-47**

1	2	3	4	5
I strongly disagree	I somewhat disagree	I somewhat agree	I agree	I strongly agree

How would you describe your experience in terms of "church life?"

Do you feel it is healthy and growing? What would make it better?

What is your methodology for inviting others into your community of faith?

3. **I am a part of a community of faith where no one has to walk alone**

[2] Carry each other's burdens, and in this way you will fulfill the law of Christ. **Galatians 6:2**

1	2	3	4	5
I strongly disagree	I somewhat disagree	I somewhat agree	I agree	I strongly agree

What does it feel like when the Lord uses you to help someone carry their burden?

When do you know when to help someone and when to include other members of the body of Christ to help?

How would you teach the person you disciple to carry the burden of others?

4.   I believe that disciples of Jesus are to instruct one another

I myself am convinced, my brothers, that you yourselves are full of goodness, complete in knowledge and competent to instruct **one another. Romans 15:14**

1	2	3	4	5
I strongly disagree	I somewhat disagree	I somewhat agree	I agree	I strongly agree

Who do you trust in your community of faith to instruct you?

Who in your community of faith trusts you to instruct them?

In your mind, how is trust developed in a community of faith where believers can learn from each other?

5. **I believe that it is my calling to encourage one another and build each other up**

Therefore encourage **one another** and build **each other** up, just as in fact you are doing. **1 Thes. 5:11**

Let us not give up meeting together, as some are in the habit of doing, but let us encourage **one another**--and all the more as you see the Day approaching. **Hebrews 10:25**

1	2	3	4	5
I strongly disagree	I somewhat disagree	I somewhat agree	I agree	I strongly agree

Typically, who do you usually seek to encourage and build up?

Typically, who usually seeks to encourage and build you up?

What kinds of things can you share that bring a richer sense of mutual encouragement when your community of faith meets together?

More Thoughts And Action Steps On Community:

1. Write a clear and precise description of what it will mean for you to grow in community this year.

2. Then, make a list of the specific goals you need to experience for growth in community (You are now going from "what it means for you" to "what will make it possible" for you to achieve success)

3. With each specific goal you list above, list the steps you will need to achieve in order to reach your goal.

4. Then, list the tasks that will be required to take each step.

5. Then, set a schedule of beginning and completion dates for each task and step

6. Finally, who will hold you accountable to reach your spiritual goals?

SERVICE: (An Overview of What I Believe)

Church members too often expect service and never think of giving it. ~ Vance Havner

God did not save you to be a sensation. He saved you to be a servant. ~ John E. Hunter

Christian Love, either towards God or towards man, is an affair of the will. ~ C.S. Lewis

We can do no great things - only small things with great love. ~ Mother Teresa

---

I know my spiritual gifts

1	2	3	4	5
Strongly Disagree	Disagree	Somewhat Agree	Agree	Strongly Agree

I am using my spiritual gifts on a regular basis in my church

1	2	3	4	5
Strongly Disagree	Disagree	Somewhat Agree	Agree	Strongly Agree

I am comfortable serving with others

1	2	3	4	5
Strongly Disagree	Disagree	Somewhat Agree	Agree	Strongly Agree

I celebrate the opportunity to affirm others who have different spiritual gifts from my own

1	2	3	4	5
Strongly Disagree	Disagree	Somewhat Agree	Agree	Strongly Agree

I have been affirmed by others who have validated my spiritual gifts

1	2	3	4	5
Strongly Disagree	Disagree	Somewhat Agree	Agree	Strongly Agree

SERVICE: (A Biblical Inquiry For Why I Believe)

1. I am confident in knowing God gives me something very special things to do for Him

For we are God's workmanship, created in Christ Jesus to do good works, which God prepared in advance for us to do. **Ephes. 2:10**

1	2	3	4	5
I strongly disagree	I somewhat disagree	I somewhat agree	I agree	I strongly agree

Do you see yourself as someone special to God who has given you very special things to do for Him?

As you reflect back upon your service to the Lord, what acts of service that seem to be "created in Christ Jesus," stand out in your mind?

How can you guide the person who questions whether or not God has a plan of service for them?

2.   I use my spiritual gift to serve others

Each one should use whatever gift he has received to serve others, faithfully administering God's grace in its various forms. **1 Peter 4:10**

1	2	3	4	5
I strongly disagree	I somewhat disagree	I somewhat agree	I agree	I strongly agree

What is your spiritual gift?

When you have been able to serve others with your gift, how would you describe their response to you?

What would your approach be in coaching someone to share their spiritual gifts?

3. **It is my frequent practice to serve the Lord with great fervor and zeal**

Never be lacking in zeal, but keep your spiritual fervor, serving the Lord. **Romans 12:11**

1	2	3	4	5
I strongly disagree	I somewhat disagree	I somewhat agree	I agree	I strongly agree

What kinds of spiritual disciplines do you practice that enhances your spiritual fervor in serving the Lord?

When you are serving the Lord, what motivates you in your service?

What can you do to inspire others to serve the Lord with spiritual fervor?

4.   I want my life to be defined not by my personal gain, but in how I serve

[43]Not so with you. Instead, whoever wants to become great among you must be your servant, [44]and whoever wants to be first must be slave of all. **Mark 10:43-44**

1	2	3	4	5
I strongly disagree	I somewhat disagree	I somewhat agree	I agree	I strongly agree

How do you respond to those times when you are tempted to be served instead of serving?

What role does pride play in your opportunity to serve others?

What would you say to the person who is self-centered when it comes to the need to serve others?

5. **I am wiling to serve anyone the Lord places upon my path**

[35]For I was hungry and you gave me something to eat, I was thirsty and you gave me something to drink, I was a stranger and you invited me in, [36]I needed clothes and you clothed me, I was sick and you looked after me, I was in prison and you came to visit me.' [37]"Then the righteous will answer him, 'Lord, when did we see you hungry and feed you, or thirsty and give you something to drink? [38]When did we see you a stranger and invite you in, or needing clothes and clothe you? [39]When did we see you sick or in prison and go to visit you?' [40]"The King will reply, 'I tell you the truth, whatever you did for one of the least of these brothers of mine, you did for me.' **Matthew 25:35-40**

1	2	3	4	5
I strongly disagree	I somewhat disagree	I somewhat agree	I agree	I strongly agree

When you are serving those in great need, what kinds of thoughts flood your mind?

What are your typical service opportunities?

How can you teach a younger believer the tools that will help them serve those in need?

More Thoughts And Action Steps On Service:

1. Write a clear and precise description of what it will mean for you to grow in service this year.

2. Then, make a list of the specific goals you need to experience for growth in service (You are now going from "what it means for you" to "what will make it possible" for you to achieve success)

3. With each specific goal you list above, list the steps you will need to achieve in order to reach your goal.

4. Then, list the tasks that will be required to take each step.

5. Then, set a schedule of beginning and completion dates for each task and step

6. Finally, who will hold you accountable to reach your spiritual goals?

EVANGELISM: (An Overview of What I Believe)

All the church is to be made up of tellers. Not everyone is to be a missionary, not everyone a minister, but there is no Christian that's really become a Christian who doesn't have laid upon him the admonition of Paul to be a debtor. Everyone is bound to be a teller in his own place, in his own calling, according to the individual vocation which God has given him. ~ Francis Schaeffer

Personal evangelism should be characterized by sensitivity. One is talking to another person, not into a tape recorder. ~ J. Barrs and R. MacCaulay

You are a Christian because somebody cared. Now it's your turn. ~ Warren Wiersbe

I have shared the Gospel with a lost person at least once in my life

1	2	3	4	5
Strongly Disagree	Disagree	Somewhat Agree	Agree	Strongly Agree

I have the kind of living witness that allows Christ to be seen in my life

1	2	3	4	5
Strongly Disagree	Disagree	Somewhat Agree	Agree	Strongly Agree

I have a prayer list of lost family and friends that I refer to regularly

1	2	3	4	5
Strongly Disagree	Disagree	Somewhat Agree	Agree	Strongly Agree

I am confident in my ability to make a clear presentation of the Gospel

1	2	3	4	5
Strongly Disagree	Disagree	Somewhat Agree	Agree	Strongly Agree

I am not ashamed of the Gospel of Jesus Christ

1	2	3	4	5
Strongly Disagree	Disagree	Somewhat Agree	Agree	Strongly Agree

EVANGELISM: (A Biblical Inquiry For Why I Believe)

1.   When an opportunity to share my faith comes my way I try to be ready

But in your hearts set apart Christ as Lord. Always be prepared to give an answer to everyone who asks you to give the reason for the hope that you have. But do this with gentleness and respect, **1 Peter 3:15**

1	2	3	4	5
I strongly disagree	I somewhat disagree	I somewhat agree	I agree	I strongly agree

What have you done in order to be ready for the times when you are allowed to share your faith?

Can you clearly describe "the hope that you have?"

What one piece of advice would you give a younger believer who is not comfortable in sharing their faith?

2.   I am both willing and eager to share the Gospel

[14]I am obligated both to Greeks and non-Greeks, both to the wise and the foolish. [15]That is why I am so eager to preach the gospel also to you who are at Rome. [16]I am not ashamed of the gospel, because it is the power of God for the salvation of everyone who believes: first for the Jew, then for the Gentile. **Romans 1:14-16**

1	2	3	4	5
I strongly disagree	I somewhat disagree	I somewhat agree	I agree	I strongly agree

What gives you confidence when you have the chance to share your faith?

What sorts of things enter your mind as you engage with an unbeliever the claims of Christ?

Describe what you would share with the younger disciple who is eager to evangelize the lost.

3. **I am called to do the work of an evangelist, to share the good news of the gospel with the lost**

But you, keep your head in all situations, endure hardship, do the work of an evangelist, discharge all the duties of your ministry. **2 Tim. 4:5**

1	2	3	4	5
I strongly disagree	I somewhat disagree	I somewhat agree	I agree	I strongly agree

What is the work of an evangelist?

When you share the Gospel, what are some significant facts you work into the conversation?

Share how you would encourage a young believer on how they can do the work of an evangelist?

4. **I am under compulsion to share the Gospel because of the urgency to work in the harvest**

He told them, "The harvest is plentiful, but the workers are few. Ask the Lord of the harvest, therefore, to send out workers into his harvest field. **Luke 10:2**

1	2	3	4	5
I strongly disagree	I somewhat disagree	I somewhat agree	I agree	I strongly agree

Who is on your short list of the lost that you know about in His harvest?

How much initiative do you have as you seek out the lost in order to share the Gospel?

What is the key to getting more workers into the Lord's harvest field?

5.   I know that my ability to evangelize comes not from a type of method but from the power of God

[7]For God did not give us a spirit of timidity, but a spirit of power, of love and of self-discipline. [8]So do not be ashamed to testify about our Lord, or ashamed of me his prisoner. But join with me in suffering for the gospel, by the power of God, **2 Tim. 1:7-8**

1	2	3	4	5
I strongly disagree	I somewhat disagree	I somewhat agree	I agree	I strongly agree

How many evangelistic methods do you use? Which ones work best for you?

Are you aware of God's Spirit upon you when you share your faith?

What one bit of testimony would you tell the young disciple when it comes to the importance of depending upon God's power when sharing one's faith?

More Thoughts And Action Steps On Evangelism:

1. Write a clear and precise description of what it will mean for you to grow in evangelism this year.

2. Then, make a list of the specific goals you need to experience for growth in evangelism (You are now going from "what it means for you" to "what will make it possible" for you to achieve success)

3. With each specific goal you list above, list the steps you will need to achieve in order to reach your goal.

4. Then, list the tasks that will be required to take each step.

5. Then, set a schedule of beginning and completion dates for each task and step

6. Finally, who will hold you accountable to reach your spiritual goals?

DISCIPLESHIP: (An Overview of What I Believe and Why I Believe It)

I am actively involved in the Great Commission, making disciples for Jesus Christ

[19] "Go therefore and make disciples of all the nations, baptizing them in the name of the Father and the Son and the Holy Spirit, [20] teaching them to observe all that I commanded you; and lo, I am with you always, even to the end of the age." **Matthew 28:19-20 (NASB95)**

1	2	3	4	5
Strongly Disagree	Disagree	Somewhat Agree	Agree	Strongly Agree

Those who examine my life know that I am a disciple of Jesus Christ by how I live a Bible-driven life, living according to God's Word

So Jesus was saying to those Jews who had believed Him, "If you continue in My word, *then* you are truly disciples of Mine; **John 8:31 (NASB95)**

1	2	3	4	5
Strongly Disagree	Disagree	Somewhat Agree	Agree	Strongly Agree

Those who examine my life know that I am a disciple of Jesus Christ by the way I love other believers

"By this all men will know that you are My disciples, if you have love for one another." **John 13:35 (NASB95)**

1	2	3	4	5
Strongly Disagree	Disagree	Somewhat Agree	Agree	Strongly Agree

Those who examine my life know that I am a disciple of Jesus Christ by the kind of fruitful life I exhibit

"I am the vine, you are the branches; he who abides in Me and I in him, he bears much fruit, for apart from Me you can do nothing. **John 15:5 (NASB95)**

1	2	3	4	5
Strongly Disagree	Disagree	Somewhat Agree	Agree	Strongly Agree

More Thoughts And Action Steps On Discipleship:

1. Write a clear and precise description of what it will mean for you to grow in making disciples this year.

2. Then, make a list of the specific goals you need to experience for growth in discipleship (You are now going from "what it means for you" to "what will make it possible" for you to achieve success)

3. With each specific goal you list above, list the steps you will need to achieve in order to reach your goal.

4. Then, list the tasks that will be required to take each step.

5. Then, set a schedule of beginning and completion dates for each task and step

6. Finally, who will hold you accountable to reach your spiritual goals?

Follow Up Reflective Questions on Discipleship

What is a Disciple?

What is Discipleship?

Who is Discipleship for?

Why is Discipleship Important?

When Should Discipleship Occur?

Where Should Discipleship Take Place?

How will one know when true Discipleship can be considered a success?

Some great questions you can ask the person you are discipling:

Personal Interview Questions on Discipleship

A. Understanding A Biblical View of Discipleship

The goal of this section is to gather open-ended feedback of these questions.

1. A Biblical view of discipleship must include adherence to the *Great Commandments*: to love God, to love one's neighbor, to love oneself—with a great passion. Will you give some examples that illustrate your commitment to love God, your neighbor and yourself since you participated in our discipleship experience?

2. A Biblical view of discipleship must include adherence to the *Great Commission (Matthew 28:19-20)* and to the *Great Commitment (2 Timothy 2:2)*: to go, and as one is going, they are not to only passionately live out the discipled life, but to be driven with an all-consuming passion, to make obedient disciples for Jesus of all ethnic groups who will teach others also to how to live the discipled life. For you, what impact does the Great Commission and the Great Commitment make in your life? Since your participation with in our discipleship experience, describe some of your experiences in making disciples who are now making disciples too.

B. Part Two: The Seven Essential Spiritual Practices or Core Values of a Disciple

The goal of this section is to gather open-ended feedback of these questions.

1. **Grace**: Based upon your experience in our discipleship experience, how would you define this term?

   Give me an example of how grace has made an impact upon your life.

More Follow Up Questions on Grace:

How has the grace of God transformed your life?

When is it the most challenging for you to live in grace?

What kind of advice would you give the person who has great difficulty in escaping the snares of legalism and the law?

Has there ever been a hindrance that prevented you from walking in the fullness of God's grace?

How does God's grace impact on the way you feel about yourself?

Is there anything in your life that hinders you from being free from habitual sin?

How does the grace of God, in your life, keep you from falling into the performance trap?

What kind of advice would you give the person who is trapped in a life of habitual sin and cannot break free?

What is your attitude concerning how free you are in approaching God's throne with your needs?

How does having the opportunity to approach this Throne of Grace impact you on a daily basis?

What kind of advice would you give the person who is desperate and in great need of God's grace?

How do you position yourself in order to experience grace being poured out on you abundantly?

How does the connection of grace in your life magnify your faith and love?

What kind of advice would you give the person who seemed to be missing out on an abundance of grace and faith and love?

2. **Worship**: Based upon your discipleship experience, how would you define this term?

> Give me an example of how worship has made an impact upon your life.

More Follow Up Questions on Worship:

Can you recall an example of when you had to worship God by faith?

What kind of advice would you give the person who has a hard time worshiping a God he or she cannot see (and sometimes, even "feel")?

What has been the catalyst for having fidelity in your worship?

What has been the hindrance that keeps you from giving God all of your worship?

What kind of advice would you give the person who does not give God all of his or her worship?

How do you know when you are pleasing God with your worship?

What kind of advice would you give the person who sincerely wanted to know what kind of worship pleases the Lord?

How does your worship of God give you perspective of how you approach and relate to Him?

What has been your greatest challenge when it comes to approaching God in worship?

What kind of advice would you give to the person who wanted to know how God wants to be approached?

How much passion do you bring to your worship of God?

After you worship God what kinds of emotions typically fill your heart?

What kind of advice would you give to the person who wanted not to only *know* that God exists, but wants to *experience* Him as well?

3. **Bible study**: Based upon your discipleship experience, how would you define this term?

Give me an example of how Bible study has made an impact upon your life.

More Follow Up Questions on Bible Study:

What is your plan to allow the Scriptures to soak your heart?

How is your typical day best described after spending quality time in God's Word?

What kind of advice would you give the person who had no desire to spend time in God's Word?

Can you think of a recent example when you received divine guidance after spending time in God's Word?

When you approach God's Word for direction, where do you begin?

What kind of advice would you give the person who was lacking comfort and direction in life?

Can you think of a time when after reading and studying God's Word, you walked away encouraged?

What kinds of things are hindrances to you when you are discouraged which keep you from being encouraged?

What kind of advice would you give the person who needs to be built up and encouraged?

What is your strategy when it comes to keeping God's Word on the forefront of your mind?

What challenges do you face when seeking to faithfully live out what you know to be the truth of God's commands?

Can you think of time where after spending quality time in God's Word it caused you to be prosperous and successful?

What kind of advice would you give the person who has no desire to either memorize or at the very least become intimately familiar with the Scriptures?

When you meditate upon the Scriptures, what kinds of things do you think about or do?

What is your greatest challenge when it comes to filling your mind with the Word of God?

What kind of advice would you give to the person who does not know how to meditate on the Word of God?

4. **Prayer**: Based upon your discipleship experience, how would you define this term?

   Give me an example of how prayer has made an impact upon your life.

More Follow Up Questions on Prayer:

Would you describe your prayer life as one of intimacy or one of ritual and religious duty?

How do you know that the Lord is listening to your voice?

What kinds of coaching tips would you give the young believer who is still trying to find their "voice" in prayer?

What do you think it means to "pray continually?"

What would you have to do in your personal life in order to deepen your prayer life?

What one thing would you share with a new believer who is struggling to develop a life of prayer?

When you pray, do you believe your problems are bigger than God or do you believe that God is bigger than your problems?

Describe a time when God did a miracle in your life as a result of your prayer to Him.

What could you say to the believer who was skeptical in the power of prayer?

Describe the process you go through when you have to make an important decision.

When making a decision, what does it mean for you to "in all your ways acknowledge Him?"

What kind of encouragement would you give to the person who facing a fork in the road?

What spiritual lessons have you learned when your prayers appear to be unanswered; either / or when and how you wished?

When you are facing a crisis (physical, emotional, spiritual, etc.) how do you determine for what to pray?

What kind of counsel would you give the person who has been disappointed in God's "failure" to give them what they wanted?

5. **Community**: Based upon your discipleship experience, how would you define this term?

Give me an example of how community has made an impact upon your life.

More Follow Up Questions on Community:

When you "love one another", what does that typically look like? What does love look like for those who are being loved by you?

When are you most willing to love others?

How would you model loving one another to a person who has a hard time receiving love?

How would you describe your experience in terms of "church life?"

Do you feel it is healthy and growing? What would make it better?

What is your methodology for inviting others into your community of faith?

What does it feel like when the Lord uses you to help someone carry their burden?

When do you know when to help someone and when to include other members of the body of Christ to help?

How would you teach the person you disciple to carry the burden of others?

Who do you trust in your community of faith to instruct you?

Who in your community of faith trusts you to instruct them?

In your mind, how is trust developed in a community of faith where believers can learn from each other?

Typically, whom do you usually seek to encourage and build up?

Typically, who usually seeks to encourage and build you up?

What kinds of things can you share that bring a richer sense of mutual encouragement when your community of faith meets together?

6. **Service**: Based upon your discipleship experience, how would you define this term?

Give me an example of how service has made an impact upon your life.

Follow Up Questions on Service:
Do you see yourself as someone special to God who has given you very special things to do for Him?

As you reflect back upon your service to the Lord, what acts of service, that seemed to be "created in Christ Jesus," stand out in your mind?

How can you guide the person who questions whether or not God has a plan of service for them?

What is your spiritual gift?

When you have been able to serve others with your gift, how would you describe their response to you?

What would your approach be in coaching someone to share their spiritual gifts?

What kinds of spiritual disciplines do you practice that enhances your spiritual fervor in serving the Lord?

When you are serving the Lord, what motivates you in your service?

What can you do to inspire others to serve the Lord with spiritual fervor?

How do you respond to those times when you are tempted to be served instead of serving?

What role does pride play in your opportunity to serve others?

What would you say to the person who is self-centered when it comes to the need to serve others?

When you are serving those in great need, what kinds of thoughts flood your mind?

What are your typical service opportunities?

How can you teach a younger believer the tools that will help them serve those in need?

7. **Evangelism**: Based upon your discipleship experience, how would you define this term?

Give me an example of how evangelism has made an impact upon your life.

Follow Up Questions on Evangelism:

What have you done in order to be ready for the times when you are allowed to share your faith?

Can you clearly describe "the hope that you have?"

What one piece of advice would you give a younger believer who is not comfortable in sharing their faith?

What gives you confidence when you have the chance to share your faith?

What sorts of things enter your mind as you engage an unbeliever with the claims of Christ?

Describe what you would share with the younger disciple who is eager to evangelize the lost.

What is the work of an evangelist?

When you share the Gospel, what are some significant facts you work into the conversation?

Share how you would encourage a young believer on how they can do the work of an evangelist?

Who is on your short list of the lost that you know about in His harvest?

How much initiative do you have to seek out the lost in order to share the Gospel?

What is the key to getting more workers into the Lord's harvest field?

How many evangelistic methods do you use? Which ones work best for you?

Are you aware of God's Spirit upon you when you share your faith?

What one bit of testimony would you tell the young disciple when it comes to the importance of depending upon God's power when sharing one's faith?

C. Part Three: The Expected Behaviors of Those Who Are Living the Discipled Life

The goal of this section to gather open-ended feedback of these questions.

What are some of the behaviors you would look for in the lives of those who have made a commitment not to only live as a disciple of Jesus Christ but who have also committed to become a disciple maker as well?

Catalysts to Spiritual Growth

In your own spiritual life, what have been some of the catalysts that have enhanced the quality of your relationship with Jesus Christ?

What are you doing now to build upon what you have achieved?

Hindrances to Spiritual Growth

In your own spiritual life, what have been some of the hindrances that have quenched the quality of your relationship with Jesus Christ?

What are you doing now in order to overcome that which is hindering you from growing in a specific area of your spiritual life?

Personal Analysis of Disciple Making

Since you began your discipleship experience, evaluate your experience in making disciples.

What has been your biggest struggle in making disciples?

More Follow Up Questions on Discipleship:
What person has made the greatest impact upon your faith?

What did this person do (i.e., style, technique, method, etc.) that caused you to grow as a Christian? How successfully have you been in adapting what you learned in your own discipleship ministry?

Can you think of an occasion where the Lord used you to mentor or disciple another believer? In your estimation, how did it go?

What would your discipleship strategy be if a person came to you today and wanted to learn how to live the Christian life?

How important is it for you that your relationships are authentic and worth the time you invest? (See 2 Timothy 2:2)

**Essential Spiritual Growth Resources from
Something New Christian Publishers
and Quality Leadership Consultants**

Websites, Newsletter, and Blogs:

www.dennybates.com is the hub for all of our teaching and coaching resources. Check out our free downloads as well as our store.

www.thequalitydisciple.com links to dennybates.com.

www.qualityleadershipconsultants.com links to dennybates.com.

www.thequalitydisciple.blogspot.com is the teaching blog for Psalms of Discipleship.

www.facebook.com/denny.bates is my portal to social networking.

Dr. Denny Bates and Quality Leadership Tips For You is my newsletter. Featured leadership articles, devotional thoughts, and a menu of coaching and book resources.

Sign up at http://www.dennybates.com/#!contact/c3kh

You can follow me on Twitter @dennybates

Books:

Other titles from the Quality Discipleship Series:

- ❖ Passing It On…How To Make A *Quality* Disciple (E-Book only)
- ❖ How To Study And Apply The Bible To Your Life (E-Book only)
- ❖ Growing Up…Practical Bible Studies For New And Growing Christians (E-Book only)
- ❖ Building A Christian Community Of Friends (E-Book or printed copy)
- ❖ Psalms of Discipleship: Growing in Grace (E-Book or printed copy)
- ❖ Winter 2013: Living Above The Fray: Learning The Seven Healthy Leadership Principles That Will Shelter You From The Destructive Effects Of Leader-I-Tis

Retreat Journals:

- ❖ The Power – Broker's Guide To The Kingdom
- ❖ Four Legacies For A Life Change
- ❖ Three Commitments That Change A Life
- ❖ Growing In Grace: A Fresh Look At Biblical Discipleship
- ❖ Adding Quality To Your Life

Contact us for availability and cost.

www.dennybates.com/resouces

QUALITY LEADERSHIP CONSULTANTS

PROFESSIONAL COACHING, CONSULTING, AND TEACHING

Presenting Quality Ideas;
Producing Quality Leaders

Introducing Dr. Denny Bates

Professional Life Coach, Teacher, Writer, Speaker And Consultant

Why is it important for you to have a professional life coach and leadership trainer?

It has been said, "Experience is the best guide in life." The truth is *guided experience* is the best guide! Time, money, and emotional energy can be saved by linking up with a person who already understands where you are, where you want to go and has a good grasp on how to lead you there in a positive way.

What kind of guided experience do I offer?

Seasoned in both the market place and non-profit settings, I can offer you and/or your organization Quality Leadership coaching tracks with a relational emphasis. For instance, Personal Growth, Communication Skills, Building Healthy Relationships, Career Counseling / Job Performance, Life Transitions, Organizational Health; and for faith-based individuals and/or organizations, Spiritual Growth. My practical experience in both for-profit and non-profit settings, coupled with my academic and professional training, affords me the ability to offer you unique Quality Leadership services.

DR. DENNY BATES
LEADING WITH QUALITY IN MIND

"Everything rises and falls on leadership"

As a Leadership Specialist, I can help YOU in the marketplace!

✓ With years of experience working as a manager in the marketplace, I know what it takes to create a healthy organization. I can train your leaders and employees in effective teamwork and communication.

✓ I know how to help business leaders practice the kind of self-care that not only benefits them personally, but also adds value to the company.

✓ I know how to help a management team build a culture that places great value on integrity and success.

✓ I can help you and your leaders set reasonable goals and show you the tools to help you reach each one.

✓ I can help you reproduce your values, vision and passion in the lives of others.

✓ I can help you sharpen your leadership skills in a group coaching setting or one to one. As a professional life coach and leadership trainer, I can offer you the finest coaching and training resources available today as a certified coach, teacher and speaker for the John Maxwell Team.

QUALITY
LEADERSHIP CONSULTANTS

Email dennybates@gmail.com

www.dennybates.com

What Others Are Saying:

Here are a few of the testimonies of people I have had the privilege to coach:

Just wanted to let you know how much our time of coaching and leadership development has meant to me. Every time I am faced with a challenge I try to walk thru the Grace tree of wisdom. You set the example every day of the man of God I want to be. Thank you! (Corporate Manager of Medical Services)

[I've learned] to keep the main thing the main thing!! To take care of the people that God puts in front of me everyday. (Sales Manager of automotive dealership)

Denny has been my friend, pastor, colleague, mentor and confidant for almost 10 years. During this time, Denny has led me through tough waters, given me wise counsel and taught me practical ways to live out my faith while falling more in love with my Savior. (Youth Pastor)

Other than my own father, Denny has been my most trusted friend and spiritual mentor. Denny's discipleship has been truly transforming and helped me to realize the importance of investing in others as he has invested in me. (Medical Device Consultant)

I treasure my relationship with Denny because we share a common heart to help people discover all that Christ wants to do in and through them. (Disciple-Making Missionary to Eastern Europe)

I have known Denny for many years and have had the privilege to work with him on the same pastoral staff for over 5 years. During that time I have sought Denny's counsel on many issues ranging from personal struggles to theological questions. Denny has always provided me with poignant, gracious and thoughtful counsel. They say that everyone should have a mentor and I am blessed to be able to consider Denny my mentor. He has been an invaluable asset in my life and ministry. (Clinical Counselor)

My relationship with Denny has been personal, honest, and Christ-centered. Denny's common sense approach to the issues of life is always soundly based on scriptural principles. I remember discussing with Denny how I felt that I needed to do so much service for the Lord because of all the times I had failed Him. Denny gently said to me, "It's all about grace". I was reminded that there is no 'payback' plan for the Lord. (Pastor)

Having a group of peers who candidly discuss the awesome responsibility that each carries as a servant and hearing how God has responded so richly to our needs clearly demonstrates how marvelous is our God, who works in each of our lives to do His will. (Hospital Vice-President in a discipleship group for executives)

Denny and I have know each other for nearly fifteen years, we bonded shortly after he had his heart attack because of an illness I had years prior – Guillain-Barre Syndrome – that made me more aware of the right priorities I should have in life. Through this episode and having children similar in age we bonded in a unique and special way rarely achieved between men. Approximately one year ago I lost my job as a senior executive at a large international company that I had been with 26 years, during the transition period of me finding another job Denny was an extreme encouragement to me. During a time when I was wrestling between accepting a position or not and I will never forget what Denny told me "You can just accept it as God's providential care". He was right! I later humbly accepted the position as President & Chief Operating Officer for a Subsea Oilfield Manufacturing company. *(Corporate Executive)*

Denny has been a teacher / mentor / discipler / encourager / prayer partner and great friend who God has used to help me keep a godly perspective on the different times & issues of life I've gone through as I've seek to follow Jesus. Once while praying with Denny through a career move, he encouraged me to think of the gifts & skills I had and then ask what I had a passion for, and then to ask God to show me how they can fit together. From this I learned to stop putting these gifts & skills in a "Box" and limiting what God could do with them, and use them for. For the first time, as I now work for a non-profit Christian organization as a warehouse manager, I feel I'm using the gifts and abilities God has given me to fulfill His purpose at something I really have a passion for! *(Former market place worker, now Missionary who is impacting the world)*

Denny met with me at 7 a.m. every Friday for a year. He came to me knowing he would receive my weekly burdens. This is not the way any of us would choose to begin our day. He does not judge nor do I ever feel judged. He is one of the most selfless and giving person I have ever met. This is easy to say because I know he is just a man. His obedience to God sets him apart. He taught me to live by grace, be long suffering, and love my wife regardless of my excuses. *(Medical Worker, Physical therapist assistant)*

Through a lifestyle of disciple making, Denny Bates has shown me what it truly means to live out Matthew 28: 19, 20. *(Educator)*

I've heard it said that on this side of eternity that there are only two things that you can be certain of: death and taxes. I'm certain of three things; the first two and that I have a friend in Denny Bates! I asked God at the beginning of my ministry to bring solid men into my life that would disciple me, teach me and hold me accountable. Denny has been an extreme answer to that prayer. *(Church-planting Pastor)*

About Dr. Denny Bates

ABOUT THE AUTHOR: Dr. Denny Bates is the husband of Trish and the father of Andrew and Corrie. He has earned degrees from Francis Marion College [B.S.], Columbia Biblical Seminary and School of Missions [MDiv, DMin]. With a doctoral degree in personal and organizational leadership, he is well equipped to serve as teacher, life coach, mentor, disciplemaker, motivational speaker and writer. Denny has served as the Discipleship Pastor in the local church, written for an international publisher of Bible commentary as well as serving as a leader in the marketplace. By God's grace, he seeks to live above the fray and "Press on!" Visit www.dennybates.com or his devotional blog at http://thequalitydisciple.blogspot.com

www.ingramcontent.com/pod-product-compliance
Lightning Source LLC
LaVergne TN
LVHW061249060426
835508LV00018B/1553